BYGONE ALDERSHOT

Endpapers: In front of the Blackwater. Sir Charles Staveley's force from Aldershot attacking Sir Hope Grant's position on the Hog's Back.

Map of the Hundred of Crondall. This large tract of land, comprising 29,000 acres, was given to the Cathedral church of Winchester as far back as Anglo-Saxon days for the support of the bishop and monks. Prior to the Conquest it was formed into an ecclesiastical district, and placed entirely under the supervision of the rector of Crondal. The southernmost district of Aldershot contains 4,144 acres.

Bygone Aldershot

Tim Childerhouse

Phillimore

1984

Published by
PHILLIMORE & CO. LTD.,
Shopwyke Hall, Chichester, Sussex

ISBN 0 85033 548 5

Printed and bound in Great Britain by
OXFORD UNIVERSITY PRESS

*To the Aldershot Historical
and Archaeological Society
whose interest made possible
the writing of this book*

CONTENTS

LIST OF ILLUSTRATIONS

Frontispiece: Map of the Hundred of Crondall.

INTRODUCTION

THE VICTORIAN-BUILT TOWN of Aldershot is situated between two main roads to London. The south road follows the line of one of the oldest trackways in England and climbs the Hog's Back where for many miles the town can be seen nestled inside the curving loop of the county stream, which has formed the boundary of Hampshire for at least 11 centuries. This high route to London goes by way of Guildford. The other route, not often used in earlier days, traverses the harsh lands of Bagshot Heath; the distance to London by way of Staines is 35 miles. It is said of Aldershot that 'previous to 1855 it was one of the most pleasing and picturesque hamlets in Hampshire, consisting of a church, and two important houses called Aldershot Manor and Aldershot Place, a few farmhouses and a village green'. So runs the description from the *Victoria County History*.

Exactly when man first arrived in the area will never be known. In early Palaeolithic times Britain was part of Europe, and evidence of primitive man's migration northwards is found in south-east England. The earliest satisfactory evidence we have for the starting point of local settlement is found on the high ground to the west of the town.

There are no myths, no legends, nor written word to help us understand what happened in this valley concerning early man. It is from the very soil beneath our feet that we can read this story, often by archaeological excavation, and sometimes by chance. There were no legal, man-made boundaries dividing the people who lived here, and to assess this heritage properly we must consider an area bounded by Wrecclesham in the west to Ash in the east, and from the Hog's Back in the south to the dominating Caesar's Hill in the north.

High on the hills and low in the valley was everything for his requirements: flint for his tools and weapons, clay for his domestic uses, timber for his huts, and water in plentiful supply. Numerous streams drained from the hills to fill the rivers Wey and Blackwater, and there were fish in abundance. His food of wild ox, deer and fowl made this place a haven.

A parish history has perhaps only a limited interest, but when the subject is Aldershot, 'The Home of the British Army', that story is of national significance.

SELECT BIBLIOGRAPHY

Baigent, F. J., *The Crondall Records*
Branson, J. W., *The Old Parish Church of Aldershot*
Cole, H. N., *The Story of Aldershot*

ACKNOWLEDGMENTS

The majority of illustrations in this book are from my own collection of Aldershot photographs. For additional illustrations I would like to thank the following organisations who loaned photographs and the permission to copy: *The Aldershot News*; M. o D., R.A.E.; The Aldershot Football Club; The Aldershot Library.

Dennis Mustard and Darby Childerhouse are gratefully thanked for the reproductions.

A BRIEF HISTORY

The Evolution of the Landscape

THE EARLIEST EVIDENCE of man's existence in the locality has so far come from finds of Paleolithic flint implements on the plateau of Bricksbury and on the higher ground in Long Bottom. There is some evidence of occupation sites from the Mesolithic period (10,000-4000 B.C.). These sites include flint-working floors found on Heathbrow, the area of Bricksbury Camp, and others are recorded as having been found in the vicinity of Skirmishing Hill on Aldershot Common. On the Hog's Back, Neolithic flint mine refuse, typical of the mining of the South Downs, was found in the early 1920s. It is suggested that, at the end of the Mesolithic period, man started to clear woodland to provide areas for pasture or wood for fires. However, it is doubtful if man had much impact on the natural landscape in these early periods. The number of people was minute and the nomadic hunting-gathering way of life leaves few lasting traces. (*The Hampshire Heritage,* Hants. County Council leaflet.) In the Neolithic period (4000-1800 B.C.) nomadism gave way slowly to a more settled pastoral farming. Men cleared and then cultivated the most easily-worked ground of Cargate, Church Lane, Windmill Hill and the chalk slopes of the Hog's Back.

Early man has left his impressive funereal monuments in the locality. To the south-west stood the earthen long barrow at Badshot-Lea, now completely obliterated by ploughing, but most of the material evidence from the Neolithic period comes from field scatters of isolated finds of flint implements, stone axes and fragments of pottery. The most numerous prehistoric monuments found in the neighbourhood are the round barrows of the Bronze Age (1800-600 B.C.). Although only two barrows still survive within the parish boundary, many more may have been destroyed by ten centuries of ploughing. There is a concentration of seven barrows on Heath Brow, two in the North Camp area and in the past the whereabouts of several others have been mentioned.

Hillforts, long thought to be entirely the creation of the Iron Age, now appear to have their origins in the late Bronze Age. The promontory fort of Bricksbury, lying to the west of the town, has never been properly investigated, but most probably this 30-acre site belongs to this period. Abury, a minor fortification, situated a little further to the west, has been totally destroyed by forest planting and gravel working. A large site on Hungry Hill was 'over-dug' in the 1860s by the military to install a gun emplacement covering the London to Portsmouth Road. Part of this Iron Age habitation extends across the A325 and into Rowhills Copse.

Military sites from the initial phase of the Roman Occupation (A.D. 43-61) are not found in the district, and although Caesar's Camp (Bricksbury) suggests a Roman site, this prehistoric earthwork was so named by antiquarians of the last century who were only interested in Roman remains. We know from history sources that southern England was soon subdued by the Claudian forces; perhaps there was little need to maintain any military presence here. The impact of the Roman villas and their associated estates was an entirely new phenomenon for the English landscape. These villas are found mainly in the valley to the south of Aldershot. Stukely, writing in the 17th century, mentions a Roman villa at the bend in the Blackwater river. He suggests the structure stood on the Surrey bank, but at this spot on the Aldershot side there stood from the 12th to the 19th centuries a large moated manor house. The remains of this house were still visible well into the 20th century. Tradition tells us that primitive homesteads were built on the sites of earlier houses where building material was readily available. Perhaps we are yet to uncover a Roman villa.

The extensive tracts of woodland in the southern region of the locality provided fuel and clay for a large-scale pottery industry stretching from Alice Holt in the west and extending eastwards into the parish. Potsherds of Romano-British pottery have been found in Rowhills Copse, and the small ponds of which there were several visible up to 1920 were probably the pits from which the original potters dug their clay. Similar potsherds were unearthed in a pit not far from the oldest structure in Aldershot, the parish church.

Anglo-Saxon Aldershot (A.D. 430–1066)

In the early fifth century administration of the Province of Britain finally crumbled with the withdrawal of Roman troops. European settlers had been migrating to these shores since the latter part of the fourth century, but much obscurity surrounds the formative years of Saxon expansion. Historical sources, place-names and limited archaeological evidence suggest the emergence of an independent 'kingdom' in east Wessex.

By 685 the Saxon Chronicles record that a young member of a royal house named Caedwalla, 'began to contend for the Wessex Kingdom'. Like many other young exiles of royal birth, Caedwalla collected an army and fought for the lands of south-east England. He harried Sussex and killed Aethelwalth, its king, but was driven out by the dead king's generals, Bercthun and Andhun. He was still a landless adventurer when he began his attempt to conquer the West Saxon kingdom. In three years of incessant war he secured Wessex, then the whole of south-eastern England and lastly he invaded the Isle of Wight. His influence in the area is recorded in a charter by which he devoted the great Farnham estate and the surrounding countryside to religious uses. This charter, purporting to come from Caedwalla of Wessex, was fabricated at Canterbury late in the 10th century, but it can claim correctly to mention boundaries adjacent to the later King Alfred's preamble (bounds) of his estate at Crondall. Caedwalla's religious dedication prevailed in this part of England. Clear evidence of the worship of Oden or Woden is furnished by such names in the vicinity as Wanborough, possessing springs which tradition says have never frozen. Indeed, Green, in his *Making of England*, says of Wanborough that in all probability it has 'been a sacred site for every form of religion which has been received into Britain'.

In the late Saxon period (A.D. 650–1066) inland rural settlements took the form of large farmsteads developing into small villages, mainly in the river valleys and on the lower slopes of the chalk downs. The majority of present-day villages almost certainly date from this period.

Ærest of isenhyrste gate on slahðor weg, ðonon on ðone nortmæstan. weg, ðæton æðeredes hagen aet Wiðighamme; forð ðn ða mearce in oa tigelaernan; forð andlang mearce on. Gisteardesuylle; ðonon andlang mearce on ðæt wottreow aet ðaere baranfyrhðe, ðonnon on aet faester geat, sua on ðet deope del; ðonon on Icaeles aewilmas to Æðelbrihtes mearce aet Ylfetamme; ðonon ut on ðone haeðfeld on Fugelmere; sua on bromhyrst; ðæt andlang burnan on Bedecanlea ðonon ofer aelne ðaere haeðfeld up to Hnaefes seylfe; ðanan west and lang mearce to strete; ðæt west to Ceolbrihtes stane ðæt west on ða festaen dic; was on ða mearce on eferaes cumb; ðæt andlang mearce on mules fen; ðeat on Duddem broc andlang streames on Drydanford; ðæt on fearnleaford; sua in on æsc aesslew; forð andlang streames inon hrunigfealles waet; ðonon andlang streames op to Æmices oran; andlang weges to wulfruscan, ðonam forð to heaðfelheale; andlang on ðeth iggeat; ðon on Lilles beam; ðonon forð on mearce to Beonetlegaegeamere; sua on ðone haedeman byrgels; ðonan west on ða mearce ðaer Eðlstan lið on haedeman byrgels; ðæt on Badecandene, sua forð on Sibæs weg; ðonan Wulfstanes mearce aet Weargeburnun; ðon on cannen dene. west wearde; ðon on Patten dene westwearde, ðon on Heglea to Ceoleages treowse; ðon forð on ða dupan Deorraberena stoden; sua in on Witaeles mere; ðæt in on ðone tobroeaenan beorh; sua on Hamstedes wylas nortewearde; ðon eft in on isenhyrston gate.

The Saxon bounds of Crondall Hundred.

Baigent, in his *Crondall Records,* informs us of the activity in and around Aldershot for the next few centuries. In 885 we have in the will of King Alfred the first written record of the existence of the Manor and Hundred of Crondall of which the village of Aldershot is part. The bequest is as follows: 'And to Ethelm, my brother's son, I grant the vill of Aldingbourne and that of Compton and that of Crondall'. The next mention of the Hundred is apparently in the will of Aelfsige, Bishop of Winchester, 925–940. How he became possessed of the manor is not clear, but he bequeathed his 'land at Crundale after my life to Aelfeah and after his life to go to the old Monastery [Winchester] that is to the Cathedral'.

In 976, King Edgar confirmed the gift to the Monastery and minutely detailed its boundaries. It is of interest to reproduce that part of the boundary of the Crondall Hundred which appertains to Aldershot.

We take up the preamble in eastern Aldershot after Fernleyford: '. . . moving south along the River Blackwater . . . so on to Ecsesslew (Ash); thence along the stream to Runingfealle's swamp Runfold); thence along the stream up to Emice's bank (Rowhills); thence along the way to Wulfrasca's (Longbottom, Aldershot Common); thence forth to the Heathfield Hall (Bricksbury)'.

It is a remarkable fact that the continuation of the natural boundary of the river can still be seen today in the form of a bank and ditch which runs for two and a half miles across the heathland; part of this bank forms not only the division between Aldershot and Farnham, but also defines the limits of the counties of Hampshire and Surrey.

The Viking and Danish raids and invasions of the ninth, tenth and eleventh centuries have left little archaeological evidence, but the Saxon Chronicles tell us of the constant battles between the Saxons and the Northmen, many on Hampshire soil. In 894 an entry referring to battles at Reading, Basing and at Farnham reads as follows: 'They now seized much booty and would ferry it northwards over the Thames into Essex to meet their ships. But the army rode before them, fought with them at Farnham and there arrested the booty. And they fled over the Thames without any ford'.

In late spring 893, two armies landed in south-east England, of which the larger army avoided any engagement with Alfred's main force and set out on a raid which extended into Berkshire and Hampshire. It turned again towards the east by river valley routes, intending to join Haesten's army on the coast of Essex, when it was intercepted and defeated. Historians suggest that the battle took place in the valley below Caesar's Camp. The West Saxon Militia under Edward, Alfred's son, had mustered on the high ground waiting for the Danes to pass below. The men of Wessex swarmed down the steep slopes and cut the invaders to pieces. Harried for a further 20 miles the Danes were driven in confusion across the Thames in deep water and many drowned. After this battle and the resulting siege of Thorney the stalemate was ended by the offer of terms to the Danes which stipulated that they should leave English territory, but left them free to join their allies in the east. Thus peace came to Wessex for a number of years.

Although the impact of the Norman Conquest (1066) resulted in great changes in political and social life, it affected the rural landscape far less. The villagers practised the same methods of agriculture. Heathland was cleared and marshes drained, winning new arable land as had been done in the earlier centuries. Not all the settlements that existed are recorded in the pages of that great document, The Domesday Survey, nor is much light shed on the evolving local parish.

Of the manor of Aldershot nothing is heard until the middle of the 15th century. By the time of the Conquest, the parish church had become a feature of the Hampshire village and it is possible that the origins of the parish lie at least in the mid-Saxon period. The earliest suggested date for the church of St Michael the Archangel is 1170, but most probably a wooden church stood on the same spot long before this. Aldershot was a tithing in the private estate of King Alfred, and was transferred in 979 to the Monastery at Winchester. It is reasonable to suppose that the new lords of the tithing, the prior and monks, would have wished for a chapel here. We know for certain that many Saxon edifices were speedily replaced by others when they came into the hands of the Normans, who, as Malmesbury tells us, were 'delighted to erect noble buildings'. Our parish church from its earliest days has been constantly rebuilt or altered and many of the original architectural features have been lost.

About 700 years of documented history of early Aldershot is to be found in the Crondall Records. The Saxon period has already been mentioned and it would appear that at a very early date the Hundred was placed under the supervision of the rector of Crondall, but in the course of time there arose the necessity for the creation of chapels of ease in some outlying areas. Of these, Aldershot was one, although it contained certain exempted lands belonging to the monks of Waverley Abbey, a Cistercian monastery which lay to the south-west of the village.

In Norman times an unfortunate feature of the structure of the Hundred was that it imposed a dual duty on the men of the tithing, for not only had they to attend the manor court of Crondall, but a document of 1284 states that all the tenants of the Hundred owed two suits of court yearly before the steward of the Lord Bishop at the Blackheathfield, which is in the Manor of Farnham. Also the men of Crondall were bound to enclose the Bishop's Park at Farnham, both freemen and bondsmen; each one according to his own share must enclose the park, which comprised two and a half leagues of land. The struggle between the bishop and the prior and convent as to which court the Hampshire tithemen owed suit went on until 1398, when it was settled in an indenture drawn up between the two parties that the free tenants of Crondall with all the tithing men of the towns, villages and hamlets of the entire manor and lordship of Crondall, together with four men of each tithing, were bound to pay two suits yearly at the Bishop's Court at Blackheathfield.

The earliest entry in the Crondall Records pertaining to Aldershot occurs in Compotus Roll of 1248, after which date there are many entries concerning the lands, the tenants and the problems which faced the villagers in the tithing. By 1334 Aldershot appears to be the most prosperous of the local villages, paying 55 shillings and twopence, its proportion of taxation to the king as compared with about 30 and 12 shillings respectively for Cove and Farnborough.

In the course of the next 200 years the tenures and customs of the manor seem to have drifted into a state of confusion and shortly after the accession of Queen Elizabeth I the Dean and Chapter of Winchester put an end to the uncertainty by drawing up a new Customary of the Manor. This was shaped in the form of an indenture made between the two parties and dated 10 October 1567, with a series of schedules setting out the names and holdings of the various tenants. There are only two existing copies of this Customary, one in the possession of the Dean and Chapter of Winchester Cathedral, and the other in the possession of the town. From this schedule it appears that the sum total of the rents arising from the tithing was at this time £16 14s. 5d. Among the place-names mentioned which could be identified about 100 years ago, before almost every field in Aldershot disappeared for building work, were 'Claversden, The Clarke's Croft, Cargate Field, Cranmore Lane End, Dudbrook and Burchett'.

From about 1200 to 1435 the monks of Waverley Abbey administered 31 acres of grazing land for sheep, the pastures being situated to the south of the grange near the church and bounded by Boxalls Lane and Rowhills Copse. There is a reference to charcoal burning somewhere on the 'common land', and this craft, too, was carried out by those same members of the Cistercian Order.

The Black Death reached Aldershot in autumn 1348 and died out in September 1350. Robo, writing in the *English Historical Review* in 1929, summarises some striking statistics of the plague in the locality. There was great difficulty in disposing of large numbers of animals received as heriot; ten plough horses sold for as little as 13s. 8d., and cows and wethers fetched half their average prices. In those two dreadful years he states that in 40 cases there was no relative left, or no heir by blood who could take up the land. About two-fifths of the population died of bubonic plague.

The establishment of the manor at Aldershot appears to have been in 1480, the first lord being John Aubrey. The manor was in 1537 recovered by Thomas Saunders and Henry White, probably the Henry to whom Robert White of Farnham in 1517 left the reversion of all his lands in Aldershot. In 1599, Robert White died without male issue. The manor had probably been left to him by his father, Sir John White, knight, who was Lord Mayor of the City of London in 1563 and died in 1573. Robert divided the manor between his two daughters, Ellen, wife of Sir Richard Tichborne, and Mary, wife of Sir Walter Tichborne, brother of Richard. And so the manor came into the hands of the influential pre-Conquest family of the Tichbornes and for over 100 years was their home. A further tithe entry in 1621 showing the annual amounts paid under a subsidy of four shillings in the pound upon lands and 2s. 8d. on goods, granted by parliament to the king, gives some idea of the principal landowners and their status at this period.

Sir Walter's lands were assessed at £20, the remaining important landowners at between one and six pounds. Comparing this 1621 list with the information recorded in the Customary of 1567, it is remarkable how in the short space of 54 years the small farmer had become eliminated, and the greater part of the lands of the parish had fallen into the hands of the Tichborne family. The assessment on goods also shows the rapid rose of a trading community. It is interesting to note that the assessment of Sir Walter Tichborne is the highest of the 12 parishes, being equalled only by Andrew Windsor of Bentley. Were the Tichbornes benefactors to an ailing community or were they determined to control as much land as possible? A grant of the office of Keeper of the Chase and warren of Crondall was made by the Dean and Chapter of Winchester Cathedral to Sir Walter Tichborne of Aldershot on 25 November 1613. This highly-regarded post was again granted to White Tichborne and his son, James Tichborne, in 1690.

Aldershot was the scene of several engagements between the Cavalier army outpost of Basing House and the London-trained bands under Waller, who was holding Farnham for the Roundheads during the Civil War. Goring's Horse of 120 sallied forth from Basing House and attacked two troops of dragoons at Crondall and Aldershot. The Roundheads who were quartered at scattered farmhouses were surprised but some managed to escape. Either four or six men were killed and 50 men and 40 horses were captured or, as one report states, only a few escaped of three companies of Roundheads and 30 out of 160 men were taken prisoner, the rest being killed. Farnham was in a turmoil as fires burned to the east and to the north of the castle.

For the first few hundred years of the 'records' the population appears to have been more or less stable, remaining at about 200, while in 1801 it had reached the figure of four hundred and ninety-four. By 1851 nearly 900 souls were residing in the village, and a mild prosperity had come to Aldershot. The manorial system of land tenure and cultivation led to the development of four kinds of agriculture: the common arable fields with their strips, the common pasture, the common meadows, and the common waste. Aldershot common with its 'common rights' was a relic of the system by which land was cultivated in much of England long before the Norman Conquest. These 'common rights' were extinguished in 1854 when 2,610 acres of Aldershot Heath were purchased by the government to be used as military training ground. The loss of this 'common waste', lying beyond the cultivated fields, made an impact upon the village and transformed Aldershot which had been unchanged for generations. Within months two armies invaded the quiet locality, thousands of troops supported by 3,000 civilian workers commenced to gouge out of the heath an encampment of hundreds of tents and 1,200 wooden huts, while a little to the south of this turmoil a shanty town supplying the needs of an army emerged. Five years later 16,000 people lived within the bounds of the parish. Aldershot was now to be known, nationally and internationally, as the permanent 'Home of the British Army'.

Wednesday 21 June 1922 will go down to posterity as the most memorable day in the history of Aldershot. On that day the Charter of Incorporation, which raised the town to the dignity of a borough, was received and handed over by the Mayor-Elect, Mr. Arthur H. Smith, in the presence of a vast assemblage of citizens in the Manor Park. The idea of raising Aldershot to the dignity of an incorporated borough had been the aim of the Rural District Council for many years. Aldershot had grown from an insignificant hamlet to a prosperous and important community.

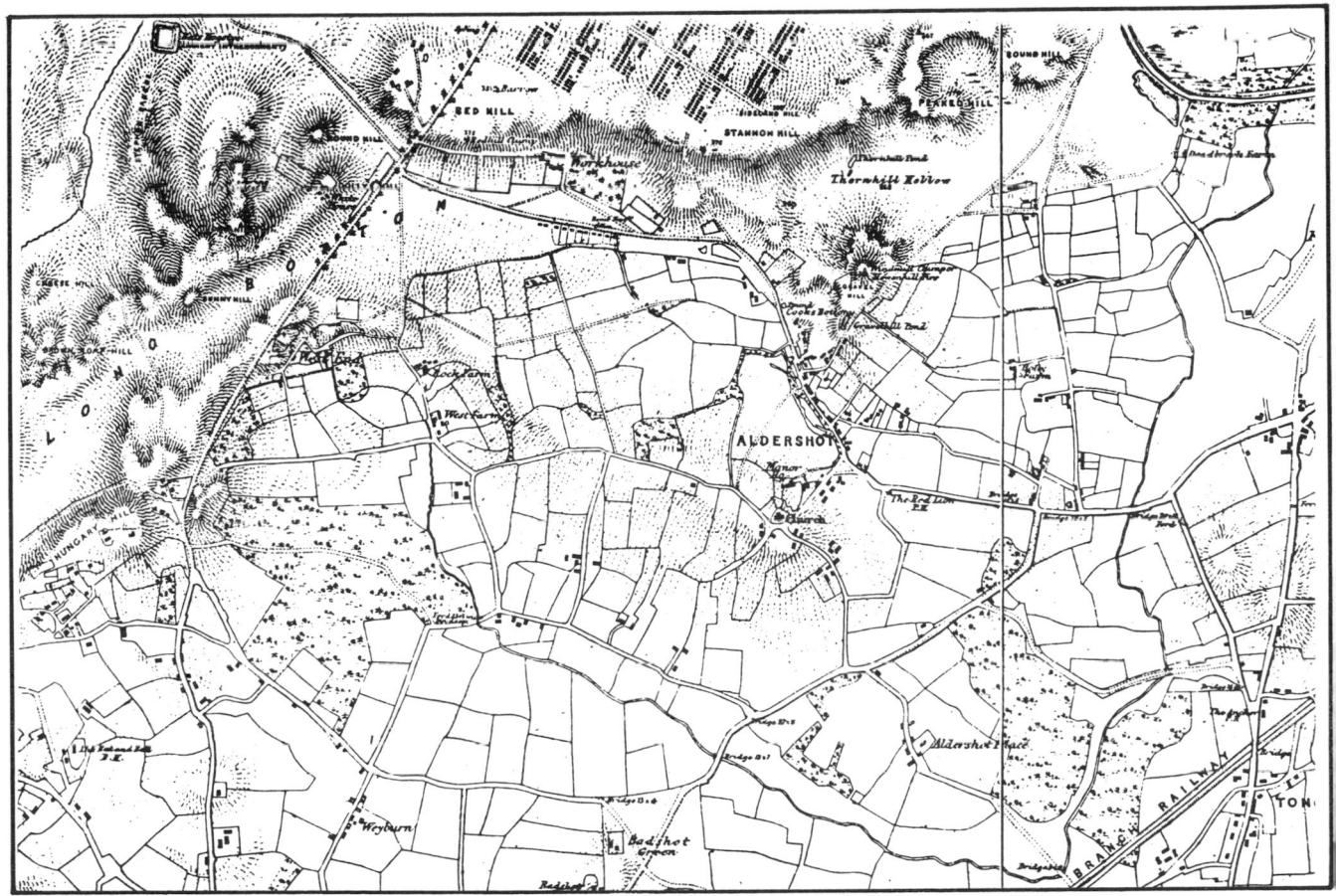

1. Aldershot in 1854 comprised a church and manor house, a few farms and two hamlets. Roughly one third of its total acreage was under cultivation, the rest was heathland which stretched from the parish boundary in the west, along the high ground to the north and almost to the River Blackwater in the east. This map shows the field system then in use.

Maps of
Early Aldershot

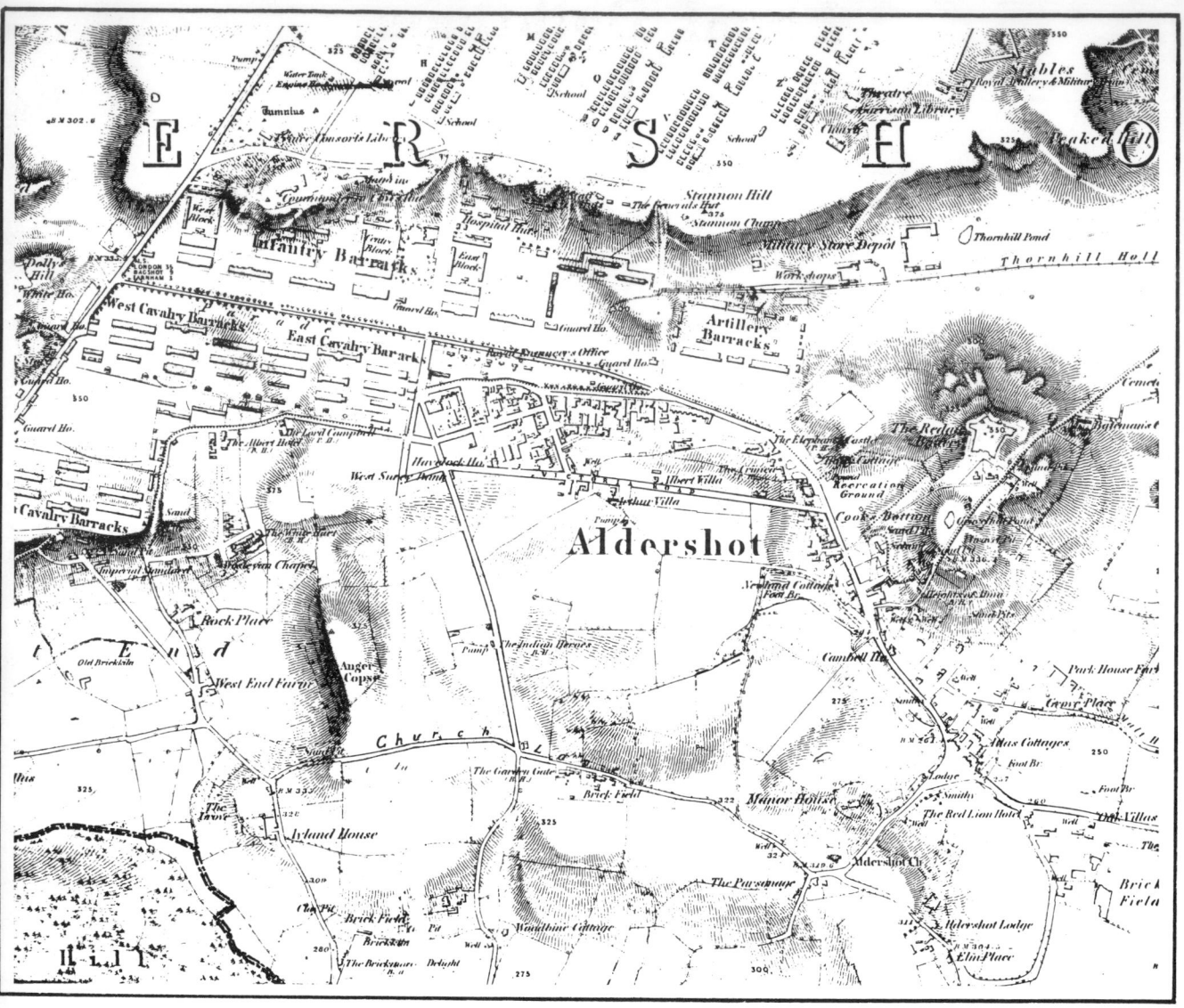

2. This map shows Aldershot ten years later, in 1864, by which time the town and permanent camp had developed.

Local Buildings

3.   The Tichbornes, as lords of the manor, deemed their mansion in Aldershot Park unsuitable for entertaining royalty. Sir Richard built this new house to the west of the village in the 1630s. It became in turn a pauper house, a school and then in 1856, the town's first military hospital. The road was built by the 'sappers' in 1857 and leads to the hutted camp.

4.   In 1870 a new manor house was built in the mouth of the parish church and within a few hundred yards of the village. Grounds befitting a manor house were created to the west. The manor house and the park were purchased by the Aldershot Council in 1919.

5. This royal residence, without doubt the most unpretentious in the United Kingdom, was designed and built in 1855 as a pavilion for Queen Victoria when visiting her troops at Aldershot. The site and design were chosen by the Prince Consort and the queen was delighted with its simplicity, the charming views from its windows, and its seclusion, and she found pleasure in painting some of these scenes during her visits to Aldershot.

6. Events moved fast in 1856. The new Aldershot town and its buildings were still not roofed over when Queen Victoria came down to stay at her new residence. In April 1856 she slept in the 'pavilion' and next morning rode over to below Caesar's Camp to inspect her troops. On 8 July the queen again reviewed the Brigade of Guards and other troops then stationed in Aldershot on their return from the Crimea.

7. Two buildings which provided valuable services for the town stood in Victoria Road. In the foreground is the Church of England Institute, which catered for soldiers of all ranks, and next door is the Hotel for the numerous visitors to the town. It was the main rendezvous for officers who were frequently posted on courses in the camp.

8. The Aldershot Cottage Hospital was opened in 1897 by the Duchess of Connaught and was enlarged progressively over the years, the money being raised by various means (*see plate 69*). This picture shows the hospital soon after the opening ceremony.

9. The Royal Aldershot Officers' Club was erected in July-August 1859 and became the centre of social life in Aldershot. The building, with a frontage of 82 ft. and 130 ft. in depth, included a large reading room, a coffee room, rooms for cards, smoking and fencing, and three billiard rooms. The Prince Consort visited the club on several occasions and gave permission for the use of the title 'Royal'.

10. A few years after its establishment, the Officers' Club was bought by the War Office from the private owner and turned over to the Aldershot Division for administration. This scene shows the court-martial of Lieutenant-Colonel Crawley in the large room of the club house.

11. The Post Office, Station Road and Victoria Road. This was designed by the surveyor of H.M. Offices of Works, London, Mr. W. T. Oldrieve, who created an outstanding building, opened in 1902.

12. This 15th-century house, photographed *c.*1950, is one of the few which survived the vast influx of thousands of troops to the town in the 1850s. Less than 20 buildings known to have existed before that time are still standing today.

13. Richard Simmonds built a roller process mill in Albert Street in the 1880s. This view is of the back of the mill which made for easy loading in the Aldershot siding. Picture 1910.

14. Fires have so often been the death knell of a business, and Aldershot had its share of the disasters. On 18 June 1910 Miles & Miles of Queen's Road was gutted. In this picture a line of neat boys and girls pose outside the building after the fire.

15. One of the major disasters for Gale & Polden came on the afternoon of 14 July 1914 when a fire started in a room on the second floor in Birchett Road and spread quickly round to the Grove side of the works. In spite of all that the fire brigades could do, both wings were gutted and the *Aldershot News* lost all its files.

16. (*right*) In 1889 Thomas White had lost his drapery shop in Union Street in a fire and some years later this fire destroyed the shop next door.

17. (*below*) The Army and the Aldershot fire brigade came to an agreement that each should assist the other if need be. In this picture, *c*.1912, a line of troops can be seen between spectators and fire.

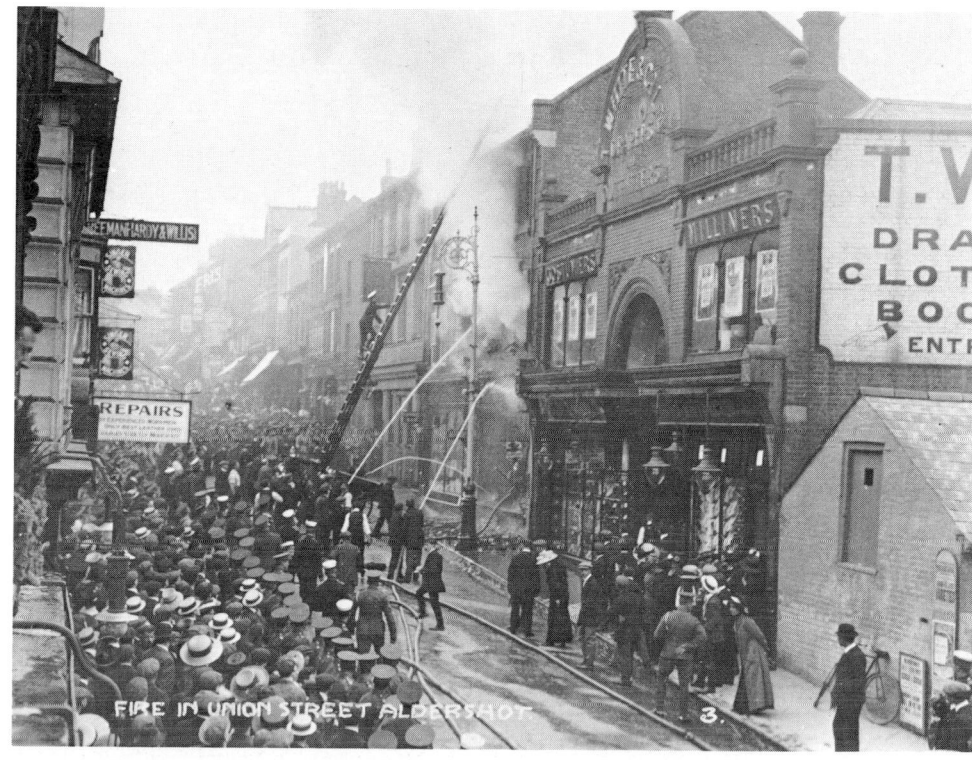

18.   This lovely house was built by Charles Baron in 1842. However, a house had stood on the same site since before the Norman Conquest, and its occupant was a little lower in status than the owner of the manor. The house stood in Aldershot Park and was finally demolished when the grounds were used for the development of a bathing pool.

Churches

19. This engraving is perhaps the earliest showing how the old parish church of St Michael the Archangel looked for about three hundred years. Great structural changes took place during the later years of the last century when a rapid population increase made it necessary to enlarge the church.

20. As a result of the great influx of people, causing the population of Aldershot to increase from 900 in 1855 to 17,000 six years later, the 12th-century parish church became far too small for its congregation. In 1870 some enlargements were made but a few years later it was obvious that a new nave had to be built on the north side of the church. This picture shows the new nave in 1908.

VICTORIA ROAD, ALDERSHOT.

21. As soon as the limits of the camp were defined the traders began building the town, which at that time catered almost entirely for the needs of the troops. The first requirements were the beer houses of which there were 40 within a few years. A certain notoriety came to the town but this was quickly combatted by the building of the churches. On the right of this picture is the Strict Baptist Church in 1862.

22. By the time a few regiments were billeted in their huts a Methodist preacher, Dr. Rule, came to Aldershot to assess the religious needs of the troops. Through his efforts an 'Iron Church' was erected in Cambridge Road in 1857. This was quickly followed by the building of the Strict Baptist and the Presbyterian churches in Victoria Road. This picture shows the Presbyterian church in 1863.

23. Almost next door in Albert Street stood this very unusual church. Designed by Westmacott, the octagonal configuration became known as the Rotunda church, or the Primitive Methodist church. It is interesting to learn that only six circular churches have been built since the days of the Knights Templar. The building was demolished in recent years.

24. When in 1857 Dr. Rule built the Cambridge Road Iron Church, he also planned the building of a Soldiers' Home. This first church of the new town, built on the edge of the camp, was soon isolated by the great wall which now enclosed the Cavalry Barracks. Twenty years later this magnificent edifice replaced the older Methodist church in the West End.

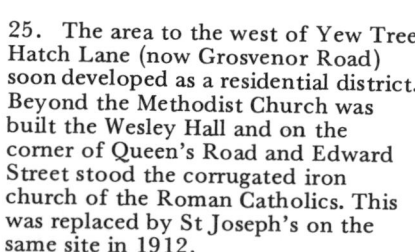

25. The area to the west of Yew Tree Hatch Lane (now Grosvenor Road) soon developed as a residential district. Beyond the Methodist Church was built the Wesley Hall and on the corner of Queen's Road and Edward Street stood the corrugated iron church of the Roman Catholics. This was replaced by St Joseph's on the same site in 1912.

26.   The Royal Garrison Church of All Saints was built in 1863 and it contains many monuments to the soldiers of the past. In the background is the magnificent statue of the Duke of Wellington on Copenhagen, which was moved here from London in 1885.

27. This attractive little chapel was built to the rear of the Church of England Institute and on top of the huge Walker Billiards Room in Victoria Road. It was dedicated to the memory of General Gordon of Khartoum in 1887. The fittings, windows, books etc. were all donated by prominent men and ordinary soldiers, and it remained one of the quiet corners of the town for nearly eighty years. It was pulled down about ten years ago.

Travel
and
Transport

28. A collection of steam engines, probably on show for one of the annual Aldershot Shopping Festivals,
photographed at the junction of St Michael's and St George's Road. The owners are unknown.

29.   The *Row Barge Inn* on the Turnpike Road had up to 1854 catered for travellers, sportsmen and bargees from the canal. By 1855 the inn became the headquarters of General Knollys and the Royal Engineers organised a timber wharf nearby for the unloading of the material from barges for the construction of the hutted camp at Aldershot.

30.   In 1906 a solitary bus route between Aldershot and Farnborough was in operation. In 1912 the new Aldershot & District Traction Co. Ltd., a development of the original operators, bought this omnibus for service on the same route.

Wharf Bridge, Farnborough Road, Aldershot

33. (*left*) The Wharf Bridge spanning the Basingstoke Canal in about 1915. By this bridge on the London to Winchester turnpike road was a wharf called, in 1790, the Farnham Eharf, or Timber Wharf, and in 1856 the Aldershot Wharf. This remained in existence until the late 1930s.

34. (*below*) As the commercial canal traffic declined a boat house replaced the timber yard on the eastern side of the bridge. The fun of punting or rowing was enjoyed by soldier and civilian alike. Part of the bridge dates from 1790.

WHARF BRIDGE, ALDERSHOT.

31. In 1914 these seven double-deckers operated between Aldershot and Farnham, Farnborough, Fleet, Deepcut and Camberley. The company's first offices were in Halimote Road. The repair shops and garages grew in size and by 1927, after 21 years of public service, no fewer than 140 buses of all types and 18 charabancs were in operation.

32. Buses, mainly Dennis's, at the Aldershot bus station in 1934. Gale & Polden's works and the Hippodrome can be seen in the background.

35. The Basingstoke Canal played an important part in the history of Aldershot. This much-renovated lock-keeper's cottage dates from about 1812.

36. A line up of traders' vehicles in St Michael's Road, at the Shopping Festival, 1922. All the familiar names of the pre-war establishments are represented. Vick Bros., John Colyer, Courage Breweries, Wasley, Darracottes, Whites etc., and at the end of the line are the traction engines of the Aldershot & District Bus Company.

37. The station *c*.1910. Horse-drawn cabs supplied good service between train and barracks. In 1870 London was within a 70-minute journey from Aldershot. By the 1930s a splendid service of fast trains cut the journey to an hour. Nowadays the journey-time has been cut to 50 minutes.

38. The electrification of the Southern Railway system was completed in 1936. This photograph shows the opening ceremony by Mayor W. J. North and Mayoress Mrs. Eva Dunn with civic dignitaries and station staff, who then travelled on the train from Aldershot to Alton when the full service came into operation the following year.

39. The Michelin 'quiet car' being welcomed at the station by Southern Rail staff after its trial run, *c*.1935.

Streets and Lanes

Aldershot, High Street, The Empire.

FRITH'S

40.   Senior officers, surveyors and engineers arrived at Aldershot in the winter of 1853 and marked out the site of the permanent barracks. The ground on the left became the Royal Engineers' Yard and determined the limits of the Camp. Speculators immediately bought up the land on the other side of the road and a temporary shanty town emerged.

High Street, Aldershot

41.   Most of the brick-built shops in upper and lower High Street had been erected by 1870. Part of the Royal Engineers' Establishment had been given over to the civil administration and the town police station with terraced cottages (left) had been built. c.1905.

42. Bustling Lower High Street in the 1940s. The Manor Park lays hidden behind the trees.

43. A more recent picture of the High Street showing right, the police houses, the police station, the court-house and the two cinemas which were all built upon the land which once belonged to the Army.

HIGH STREET, ALDERSHOT.

H.455.

44. (*above*) The town developed rapidly. Lloyd's Lane was renamed Wellington Street. The building on the right is the original *Tilbury's Hotel* where on 4 November 1857 the Board of Health held its first meeting. *Tilbury's* became the *Royal Hotel* and was finally pulled down in 1932. Under the clock is the entrance to the covered market and a 'penny bazaar'. This picture dates from 1905.

45. (*below*) Wellington Street in about 1925. The horses of earlier years are being replaced by the motor car but the hand cart still seems to be the main method of delivery.

46.   Wellington Street from Victoria Road, *c.* 1910. The scene has not changed much even today but the original names of the shop owners have gone. Next door to the London and County Bank is the Arcade entrance, Nelson & Goodrich, Halfords, Holderness, Lloyds the Chemist and off to the right is Little Wellington Street. Harrington's and Jerome's are perhaps the only remaining proprietors from this period.

Union Street, Aldershot.

47. (*above*) Many of the temporary wooden and tin shops, beer halls and miniature theatres remained in Union Street until the late 1860s. Redeveloped in 1870 as a very modern Victorian shopping centre, well-known family businesses thrived here for one hundred years. The majority of these shop-fronts remain to this day.

48. (*below*) Union Street from Wellington Street, *c.*1915. White's as a business firm is as old as commercial Aldershot. A disastrous fire which occurred in the drapery section in 1889 resulted in the building of the premises seen on the right, which contained an arcade leading through to their shop in High Street. Only four public houses were allowed to replace the many beer halls.

VICTORIA ROAD, ALDERSHOT.

49. (*above*) Victoria Road was originally developed as a residential area but because of the rapid increase in population and the demand for trade nearly every house soon established shops in what had been their front gardens. This photograph was taken about 1910.

50. (*below*) A scene which has remained unchanged for about 60 years. The entrance to the market place on the right disappeared when work began on the Wellington Centre.

51. (*above*) Grosvenor Road, 1919. Standing in one corner of the park is the town hall built in 1904. This was followed by the erection of the fire station and after World War I on 18 March 1923 H.R.H. The Duke of Gloucester unveiled the Aldershot War Memorial in the municipal gardens.

52. (*below*) In 1855 about 200 yards of track, known as Yew Tree Hatch Lane, stretched from where the *Queen Hotel* now stands to about the junction of Grosvenor Road and Queen's Road. From that point Grosvenor Road was developed along a line of hedges and became the link road between the camp and the lower road to Farnham. This picture was taken in 1930.

53. Although Church Lane East was one of the original roads of the village it was not fully developed until about 1900. This scene is looking towards the church in about 1913.

CHURCH LANE EAST ALDERSHOT.

CARGATE AVENUE, ALDERSHOT

54.   The fields of Cargate, lying to the west of the town, were developed in the 1880s as a high class residential district. Behind the trees were many fine examples of architect-designed houses. Many of these were demolished after World War II; the remainder survive as the area has been declared a conservation zone. This photograph was taken about 1915.

55.   Looking towards Hospital Hill from Barrack Road, 1900. Whenever a contingent of soldiers or a high-ranking person passed along Wellington Avenue the civilian population would respond and many hundreds of sightseers would soon gather. The military police would block an intervening road and a traffic jam would ensue. East Cavalry gates are on the left, and the Royal Engineers' Yard on the right.

56. Ayling Lane remained in its original setting until the late 1920s. The bank on the left is an old boundary which probably divided Rowhill's copse from the fields on the east. This picture was taken about 1937.

Leisure and Pleasure

57. Taylor brought his biograph to Pickford Street in 1899. Among the pictures shown were Sir Redvers Buller, G.O.C. Aldershot, leaving for the Cape War, and stirring military scenes of the departure of the troops from the camp. The Picture Palace arrived some ten years later and is still used as a cinema. Station Road, 1914.

58. When the Army released the Royal Engineers' Yard (now the Princes Gardens) for purchase by the council, the first building on the site was the Empire cinema. Here the R100 airship passes over the partly constructed cinema in 1929.

59. Until the coming of the cinema, the main places of entertainment were the Hippodrome and the Theatre Royal. Many famous people played here and during the two World Wars these houses were packed to capacity by the troops. The high building at the rear in this photograph of the Theatre Royal in 1945 is the stage area which housed the many necessary screens and backdrops for the shows. James Mason made his debut as an actor in this theatre.

60. (*right*) The year 1913 saw the building of the Hippodrome at the corner of Birchett Road and Station Road and it was considered one of the finest buildings of its kind. During the 50 years of its existence nearly every celebrity and theatre company entertained here.

61. (*below*) 'The Lads of the Village', a unique organisation which raises money in the locality. Here they are seen singing Christmas carols on the stage of the Hippodrome in 1934.

Aldershot Bathing Pool, Children's Corner.

62.   A popular addition to the amenities of the town was the opening in the spring of 1930 of one of the biggest open-air swimming pools in the country. The pool is situated in beautiful and picturesque surroundings, covers some ten acres and offers many other facilities.

63. Day trips to the coast became popular during the late '20s and '30s. A 14-seater charabanc from Aldershot & District is seen here setting off for the day.

64. The purchase of an ancient field known as 'the Parish Clerk's Land', now known as the municipal gardens, gave to the people of Aldershot a park of grand proportions within a few yards of the main shopping centre. The planting of special trees was performed in 1905 by civic dignitaries at a ceremony known as 'arbour day'.

Aldershot F.C. 1932-33.

E. Gerrard   R. Wade   W. Robb   J. W. Dougall   T. Lawson   R. Wilson
J. Proud   J. Thom   A. Smith   J. Lane   L. Firbleck   J. Middleton

67. (*above*) The first batch of professional footballers to undergo a war-time course at the Aldershot School of Physical Training passed out in October 1939, just before the outbreak of war. Many of these famous footballers played for the town during the war years, and of course, the team was the best in the country! Middle row left is Joe Mercer, next is Bloxham of Millwall. Back row left is Davidson of Middlesborough and Scotland, and back row right is W. G. Berry of Brentford.

65. (*opposite above*) This military-owned field, the nearest to the original village, was after World War I entirely re-made as a relief measure to provide work for unemployed men. Since the formation of a professional football club in the town it has been the home of 'The Shots' (from 1927 onwards). This picture shows the 'professionals' in action, while steam from a passing train billows across the pitch.

66. (*opposite below*) After five years as a professional side, playing in the Southern League, Aldershot was elected to the Third Division South in 1932. The team reached the fifth round of the F.A. Cup only to be beaten 2-0 away to Derby County. Willie Robb, the popular goalkeeper, would discuss the day's play with the customers of the *Wheelwrights' Arms* in Waterloo Road on the same evening after a home game.

Occasions and Personalities

68.   Perhaps it was the memory of the Prince Consort's 1851 Exhibition, or maybe it was because the officers of the camp decided that a trade fair might be good for camp and town, which resulted in an Industrial Exhibition being held in the Royal Officers' Club in 1864. Little is known of the event but this engraving shows a crowded hall of interested visitors. The pictures round the walls are of the military collections.

69. Young volunteers collecting for hospital funds outside Cambridge Road grocery shop, *c.* 190

70. The photography business in the town thrived, as there was so much to record. This posed scene was taken by J. W. Jacklet of Victoria Road in 1909.

71. Butcher, Harry King, standing in the doorway of his shop in High Street. This family business, situated next door to the *Volunteer*, served the area for two generations.

72. (*above*) On 7 August 1913 local hero, Colonel Sam Cody, offered a flight to W. H. B. Evans, the Oxford University and Hampshire cricket captain. At Ball Hill, not far from the Basingstoke Canal, the machine suddenly crashed. Cody and his passenger were both killed. Here the funeral procession makes its way to the military cemetery.

73. (*below*) Thousands of people were in Aldershot on that day, to honour Cody, the popular American showman, the first man to fly in this country. Wreaths were sent from the king and other members of the royal family, from the 'flying community' and from ordinary people. All these flowers were piled over his grave.

74. (*right*) Armistice Day at the War Memorial in about 1926.

75. (*below*) The tree-lined Wellington Avenue on Sunday mornings offered a gay sight especially in fine weather, when the regiments in full-dress uniform marched along its bright roadway on their way to and from church. Here the Cavalry regiment with swords is approaching 'The Red Church', with the Badajos barracks on the left. This photograph taken in 1903.

76. When King Edward VII came to the throne he ordered all regiments to walk-out in full dress. The familiarity of the uniforms encouraged more and more sightseers to the Sunday morning parades. After 'fall-out' the bands would entertain on the barrack squares with a selection of music. After the parade, 1909.

77.   General Hon. Sir Francis Gathorne-Hardy and the Mayor of Aldershot take the salute outside the church of St George, Queen's Avenue, during the St George's Day Scouts' parade, 1936.

78. One of the best methods of collecting money for the Cottage Hospital was the annual carnival. This popular, well-organised event was started in 1894 and included a torchlight procession at night. The carnival as a social function became a regular institution in the town. This picture shows the winning tableau float 'Chess' in 1911.

79. Miss Laura Palmer, daughter of Lord Wolmer, opens Aldershot Shopping Festival, October 1936. Present are the Mayor, Alderman W. J. North, the Lady Mayoress, Mrs. Kenneth Dunn, Lord Wolmer, members of the Chamber of Commerce and many other dignitaries.

80. Since the days of the Crimean War, there had always been one Guards Battalion stationed in Aldershot. The honour of leading the parade at the Charter Day celebrations on 21 June 1922 went to the 2nd Battalion Grenadier Guards. This picture was taken on the corner of Redan Hill and the High Street, opposite the *Frickers Hotel*.

81. The Charter Day ceremony. On 23 March 1922 the Charter for the Incorporation of Aldershot as a municipal borough was signed by King George V. Never in its history had Aldershot seen such a spectacle as that provided when the long procession of military units and civil organisations entered the arena of Manor Park. Here, on 21 June 1922, the Charter is being handed over. The main personalities have been named on the original photograph: the man on the left facing forwards is the Right Hon. J. B. Seely, Lord Lieutenant of Hampshire; the man in the light suit is Mr. R. J. Snuggs, Chairman of Aldershot U.D.C.; the man in the dark suit is Mr. Arthur H. Smith, Mayor Elect; and just behind him to the right is Lieutenant General Sir T. L. N. Morland, G.O.C. Aldershot Command.

82. The show which won world-wide renown and was a great feature of the life of both camp and town was the annual Aldershot Tattoo. By 1939 this attracted more than half a million spectators to Rushmoor arena. The Grand Finale, 1929.

83.   (*above*) Thousands of school children were invited to the final daylight rehearsal of the Aldershot Tattoo. H.R.H. Princess Elizabeth and H.R.H. Princess Margaret, accompanied by Lt. Gen. Sir John Dill, arriving at the 1938 daylight rehearsal.

84.   (*opposite*) *The Volunteer*, 1897. The staff and customers are posing outside the inn during Queen Victoria's Diamond Jubilee celebrations.

85. (*above*) A memorable
and impressive occasion, held
at Rushmoor Arena in July
1935, was the Silver Jubilee
Review of King George V.
The king wore the khaki
uniform of a field-marshal,
and his four sons rode
mounted in attendance on
him, wearing the uniforms
of their regiments.

86. (*left*) One year later the
king, who so often stayed in
Aldershot, was dead. The
caption on the wreath
recorded 'With profound
sorrow, and in grateful
memory of their Beloved
King. From the Mayor,
Mayoress, and Citizens of
Aldershot'.

87.   The Mayor of Aldershot, Alderman W. J. North, reading the Proclamation of King George VI from the entrance of the municipal building in 1936. The man on the right hand of the Mayor is Mr. D. Llewellyn Griffiths and the mace-bearer is Mr. Davis.

88. *(above)* For the coronation of King George VI street parties were the order of the day. Here the people of Crimea Road celebrate in 1937.

89. *(below)* The mayor calls in for a cup of tea.

Military Aldershot

The greatest change throughout all the centuries of its existence came to the village on 11 January 1854 when Lord Hardinge reported to the government that the owners of the Aldershot heathlands were prepared to sell its share of 25,000 acres at £12 per acre. The outbreak of war with Russia had far-reaching effects on the plans already drawn up for a permanent camp at Aldershot, and the building plans were extended to include brick-built barracks. At first many tents housed the soldiers and the camp was laid out to comprise two separate wooden-hutted camps set out in symmetrical lines, North Camp lying to the north of the Basingstoke Canal and South Camp on the Aldershot side. These two camps comprised of some 1,600 huts which cost £150 each.

At this period the two camps consisted of a series of blocks, which meant the collation of huts included under one letter. Each block consisted of 40 huts and was intended to accommodate one regiment. However, only 22 huts were allocated for the men, each housing 22 soldiers; of the remaining huts four were for the officers, 14 for stores and regimental uses, one was set apart for field officers and one for mess. There were 920 huts in South Camp and 680 in North Camp. Each regiment was about 484 strong. The first troops to arrive were 103 officers and men of the 94th Regiment who marched to Aldershot from Windsor. They were followed shortly afterwards by two militia battalions and so this first permanent camp became the 'Home of the British Army'.

90. Jubilee Review by
Queen Victoria, 21 June
1887. Never had any military
spectacle been held in England which could compare
with that of the review of
60,000 troops held in the
Long Valley to celebrate
Victoria's 50 years as queen.
On parade were members of
the royal houses of Europe,
Eastern rulers and the lords
and ladies of the realm.

91. The 'Royal Salute' was given by the 60,000 troops lined up in brigades stretching from the canal in the east to the slopes of Caesar's Camp in the west. Many thousands of civilians braved the heathlands to attend this colourful spectacle. A group of firs were planted on Caesar's Hill to mark this occasion. This picture shows the queen leaving the review ground.

92. (*above*) Q Lines, North Camp in about 1894, looking from a spot which later became Redvers Buller's Road on the corner of Tournay barracks.

93. (*below*) After 50 years of use the wooden huts give way to the red brick barrack blocks. The transition period of the early 1900s caused upheavals in regimental movements. This shows the scene from Corunna Barracks to Gibraltar Barracks, Stanhope Lines. Two rows of huts still remain. Queen's Avenue is on the extreme right. White-coated infantrymen in pill-box hats stroll between the barrack blocks.

94. Officers of the 4th Battalion Bedfordshire Regiment at Aldershot in about 1894. The landscape shows a typical training area.

95. This remarkable picture inside a mess hut was taken in 1896. The huts were then 40 years old and due to be replaced by brick-built barrack blocks. The contrast in the picture is amazing. The sky can be seen through the gaps of the bare wooden sides but the mess table, with its silverware and white tablecloth, is of a standard fit for royalty.

96. The original 'time gun', c.1860. An important feature of life in the camp in the early days was the firing of a signal gun at midday, and again at 9.30 p.m., as a signal for the men to return to their quarters before 'lights out'. The gun was located on the site of the Cambridge Hospital until 1873.

97. When the hospital was built the gun was removed to near the entrance of the military cemetery on Thorn Hill, but Gun Hill Road remains and now leads to the Military Hospital. This picture shows the scene c.1910.

P 40815 - Time Gun, Aldershot.

HOSPITAL HILL
ALDERSHOT.

Government House, Aldershot (No. 1)

100. (*above*) Government House was completed in 1883. Sir Daniel Lyons occupied it for a year, during which time he spent £1,000 on it. It has also been occupied at various times by Sir R. Allison, Sir Evelyn Wood, the Duke of Connaught, General Buller, General Hilyard, Earl French, General Smith-Dorrien and Earl Haig. It was burnt down in 1903 and rebuilt the same year.

98. (*opposite above*) The replacement gun was installed on Thorn Hill and was used until 1914. It was fired via the electric telegraph from a signal at Greenwich. Thus camp and town had the correct time long before other towns in Britain.

99. (*opposite below*) These two three-storey infantry barracks were built in 1856-9. They were said to be the finest design of their kind in the world and accommodated one commanding officer, two field officers, 44 officers and 1,400 men. Pictured here is the Talavera Block in about 1910, which was demolished during the 1960s 'new camp' planning. Note the huge canopy of glass which sheltered the parade ground on wet days.

BIRDS-EYE VIEW, STANHOPE LINES, ALDERSHOT.

101.   View of the Stanhope Lines from Redan Hill in 1910, showing the great number of trees planted on what was poor, sandy soil before landscaping.

102.   The long panorama of the infantry barracks, looking west towards the Red Church. These barracks were named after three of Wellington's Peninsular War victories, Talavera, Salamanca and Badajos. The combined permanent barracks were known as the Waterloo Lines. On the right are the Royal Artillery lines.

FIELD-MARSHAL SIR J. FRENCH

FIELD-MARSHAL EARL ROBERTS

GEN. SIR SMITH-DORIEN.

GEN. DOUGLAS

FIELD-MARSHAL EARL KITCHENER

MAJOR-GEN. MURRAY

GEN. BADEN-POWELL

GENERAL SIR IAN HAMILTON

GEN. HAIG

103.   The national heroes. All the famous soldiers served at Aldershot, most of them as General Officer Commanding the Garrison, and they became familiar figures throughout the camp and town.

104. Perhaps the most popular of these famous soldiers was General Sir Redvers Buller.
On his return from the South African War there was a civic-military reception never before
seen in Aldershot, this particular day being remembered as 'Buller Day' for many years
afterwards. General Buller is buried in Winchester Cathedral.

105. Prior to the Crimean War small regimental hospitals existed in local garrisons. In 1873 these regimental hospitals, with the exception of the Foot Guards' and Household Cavalry's, were abolished and placed under garrison establishments. At the same time all medical officers were regrouped as the Army Medical Department. This led to the building of the very large military hospital at Aldershot.

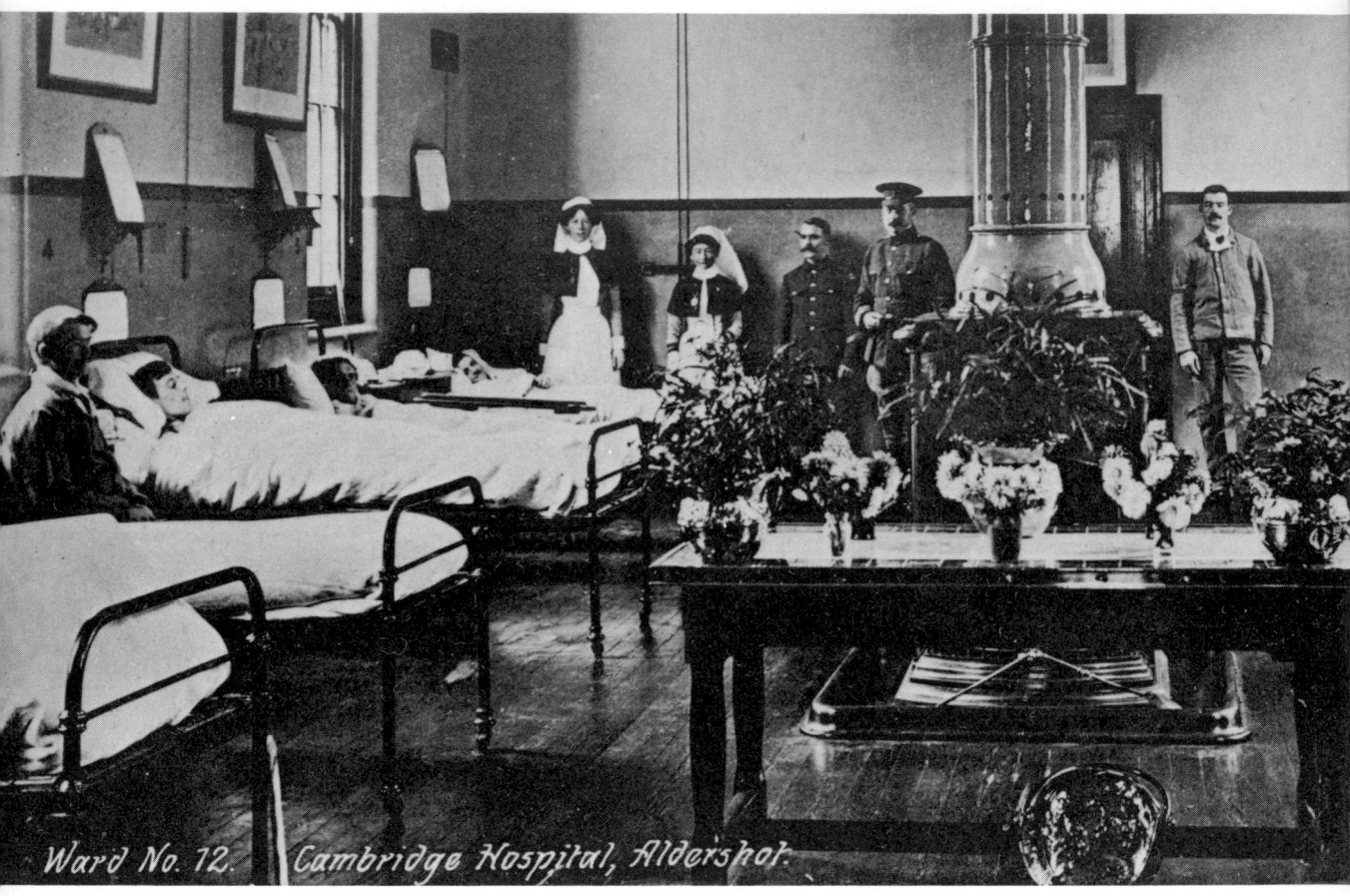

Ward No. 12.   Cambridge Hospital, Aldershot.

106.   The Cambridge Hospital, named after the Duke of Cambridge, was opened for admission of patients on 18 July 1879 with 260 beds available for the sick. This shows the inside of one of the wards in 1911.

107.   (*above*) Hidden among the silver birches the Royal Engineers inflate a balloon. This sight had been seen in and around the camp since 1889 when the Royal Engineers first began balloon training here. Note the new style fatigue dress, broderie cap and bandoliers visible on this 1904 photograph.

108.   (*below*) Royal visitors inspect balloon inflation, *c.*1906. The Royal Engineers were the forerunners of the R.A.F., starting with the 'Balloon Section', then the Air Battalion, which later became the Royal Flying Corps, and finally the R.A.F. of today.

109.   The first parachute jump over Aldershot on August Bank Holiday, 1899, was made by the Frenchman, M. Caudron. Here, sappers control a British-made parachute.

110. (*right*) An American, Samuel Franklyn Cody, in his early life was associated with a cowboy troupe and the stage. He appeared at the Theatre Royal, Aldershot, with his troupe in 'The Klondyke Nugget' just before the turn of the century. He spent the money he made on experiments with man-lifting kites.

111. (*below*) A Cody kite breaks adrift from its mooring wire and crashes inside the military stadium.

112. Cody's kites were so successful that he was employed by the War Office at Aldershot in the Balloon Section Royal Engineers as a kite instructor. This popular man settled in Victoria Road and often lectured in the town. In later years he built a number of successful aeroplanes and was the first man to fly in this country in 1908. Here he is seen with sappers on Aldershot Heath in 1904.

113. Aldershot was at the hub of military aviation and whenever a balloon, a kite or an aeroplane landed in the locality the people would flock to witness the latest invention. This Bleriot probably forced landed on Queen's Parade in about 1911.

114. Painting by Edouard Detaile of Edward, Prince of Wales, later King Edward VII, and Prince Arthur, Duke of Connaught, G.O.C. Aldershot, at a royal inspection in 1895.

115. (*above*) King Edward and Queen Alexandra, accompanied by the Queen of Denmark, driving to inspect 20,000 troops on Laffans Plain, 12 June 1907.

116. (*below*) There were three main sites for reviews. They were the common, the Queen's Parade and Laffans Plain. This picture shows the Royal Horse Artillery march-past at Laffans Plain in about 1903.

A REVIEW, LAFFANS PLAIN, ALDERSHOT.

117. A few years later the motor car replaced the carriage as a mode of transport. This picture shows the King, Queen and Princess Mary at Aldershot in 1913.

The King & Queen & Princess Mary at Aldershot 1913.   F. Scovell.   55.

GRAND NAVAL & MILITARY PAGEANT. "SONS OF THE EMPIRE, THEN (1807) AND NOW 1907"
ALDERSHOT MILITARY TOURNAMENT

118.   Ninety years ago a torchlight tattoo was held in honour of a visit of Her Majesty Queen Victoria. This superb spectacle was continued as the Aldershot Military Tournament or more popularly the Military Fete. In 1907 the main event was billed as 'Sons of the Empire, Then and Now, 1807-1907'. The performers came from all parts of the British Empire and the magnificent uniforms were furnished by the governments of the colonies represented. The tattoo was held in the grounds of Government House in North Camp.

119. (*right*) This is a rare picture of an airship and a British Army aeroplane over Aldershot, *c.*1910. Troops would use such occasions to simulate air attacks on marching columns.

120. (*below*) Looking down Queen's Avenue towards the town. The lines of chestnut trees were planted in 1899. Two of the tree barrack blocks have survived and are now the Military Historical Trust Museum.

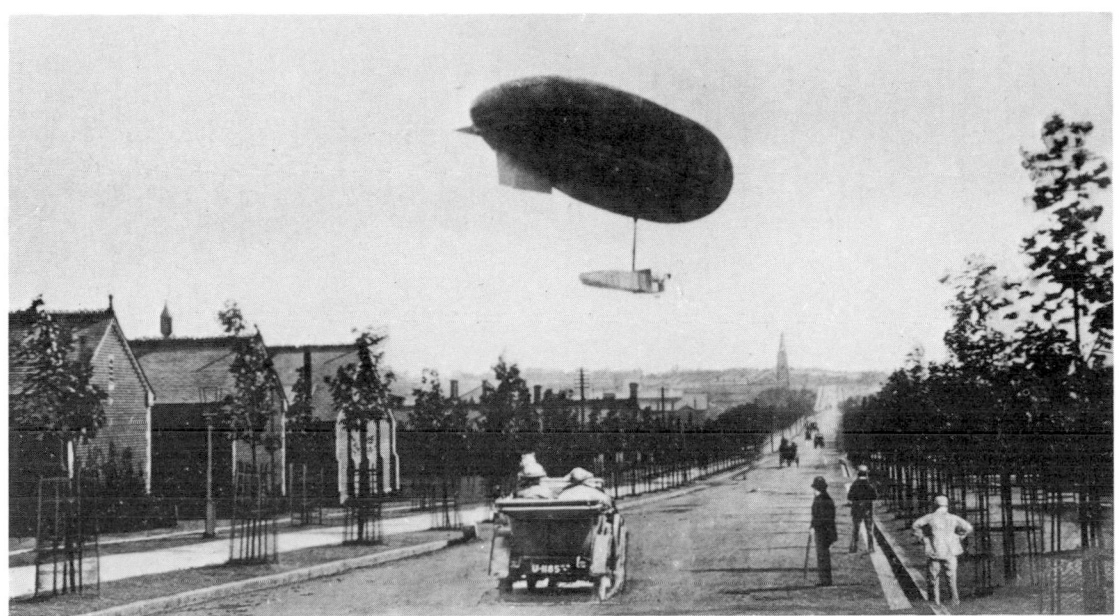

121. The Army Cup was instituted by the Army Football Association in 1888 and was open to all military teams in the United Kingdom. In 1907 the Depot Battalion Royal Engineers beat the Bedfordshire Regiment by three goals to nil.

122. In 1860 Major Hammersley of the 14th Foot, and 12 specially selected N.C.O.s, now affectionately known as 'The Apostles', were assembled at Aldershot Camp and sent to Oxford to undergo a six month course of physical training. On completion of the course, a School of Instruction was set up in Aldershot and the first gymnasium in the Army was built here in 1861.

123.   Inside the gymnasia the young men train to a peak of fitness. Teams from the Physical Training Corps entertained at the Royal Military Tournaments from the latter years of the last century and many a potential boxing champion was found in the ranks. These magnificent large halls were often used for the regimental balls and became one of the most popular features of town and camp.

124. (*above*) King George V and Queen Mary visit the swimming baths in 1912. Swimming as a physical exercise was first adopted by the army which encouraged this form of recreation long before the civil administration recognised its benefits.

125. (*below*) Inside the baths, 1913.

126. Horses, horses, everywhere: horses in training, horses to entertain, horses on parade and horses in combat. Aldershot was not a 'one horse town' and many a young lad was posted here to suddenly find himself with his own beautiful animal. This picture shows cavalry horses at Beaumont barracks in 1911.

127.   One of the reasons why Aldershot was chosen as a training ground is that there are many thousands of acres of heathland in its vicinity. Often as many as 3,000 horses would be man-oeuvring in column, in file or just grazing on the common. This scene shows horses learning to swim in the 'horse pond'.

128.   In addition to the cavalry units, every regiment had its horse-drawn transport. With all this traffic the heath was trampled and churned into dust. However, after 90 years of constant use, the land slowly returned to its natural state of heather and gorse, and later silver birches, when the Army became mechanised and the heath was used less and less. The area shown in this picture is below Caesar's Camp and was the habitation of early man. In spite of this activity, it is believed that this thin layer of soil conceals many archaeological remains such as barrows, Neolithic flint chipping floors and ancient coins.

129. Under canvas, on the march and in the field, Tommy was supplied with hot rations and tea, carried in these mobile kitchens. Perhaps the most famous remembered by the troops up to World War II was the Aldershot Oven, depicted in the foreground of this photograph.

CRANLEIGH SCHOOL
2ᴺᴰ CADET Cᵒʸ
2ᴺᴰ V.B. THE QUEENS
R.W. SURREY REGᵗ.

130. The annual volunteer camps included the Public Schools' Cadet Companies. The slouch hats worn by some of these boys from Cranleigh School, at camp in 1901, are a reminder of the Boer War when all the regular battalions left the camp for South Africa.

131. (*above*) The Sunday church parades at St George's, Queen's Avenue, were held at a slightly later time than those at the Royal Garrison Church in Wellington Lines. This did enable sightseers to attend the second series of parades. Queen Victoria laid the foundation stone in June 1892 and the church was dedicated the following year.

132. (*below*) The Scottish Regiments attended both St George's and St Andrew's which was close by.

Scottish Church Parade, St. Georges Church, Aldershot

133. (*above*) Aldershot was the home of the 1st and 2nd Divisions and it was from here that the British Expeditionary Force set out for France in 1914. This picture shows new recruits, still in 'civvies', being inspected by King George V. Nearly every new battalion raised passed through the camp in World War I.

134. (*below*) The royal party inspects the 'mobile forces' at Salamanca Barracks, 1932. The King often spent a week in Aldershot watching the manoeuvres and taking the salute at the Royal Review.

135. On 15 September 1940 the Local Defence Volunteers re-formed as No. 6 Company of the 25th Battalion Hampshire Home Guard. There was no lack of recruits; the military families which had settled here soon swelled the company to over six hundred strong. The company maintained a guard around the outer defences of Farnborough Aerodrome.

136. (*below*) Aldershot town and camp celebrated its centenary in 1954. Once again the Guards marched through the streets of Aldershot. This is Barrack Road with a contingent turning into the High Street.